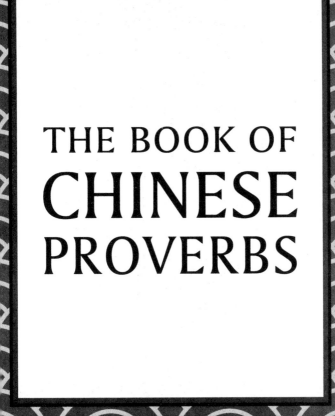

THE BOOK OF
CHINESE
PROVERBS

THE BOOK OF
CHINESE
PROVERBS

A COLLECTION OF
TIMELESS WISDOM, WIT,
SAYINGS & ADVICE

Compiled by
Gerd de Ley

Hatherleigh Press is committed to preserving
and protecting the natural resources of the earth.
Environmentally responsible and sustainable practices are
embraced within the company's mission statement.

Visit us at www.hatherleighpress.com and register online
for free offers, discounts, special events, and more.

THE BOOK OF CHINESE PROVERBS

Text Copyright © 2019 Hatherleigh Press

Library of Congress Cataloging-in-Publication Data is available.

ISBN: 978-1-57826-826-9

COVER DESIGN AND INTERIOR DESIGN BY CAROLYN KASPER

Printed in the United States

10 9 8 7 6 5 4 3 2 1

Contents

Introduction

OF THE WIDE VARIETY OF PROVERBS I've gathered in my career, perhaps the most satisfying—and indeed edifying—experiences came from my Chinese research. Coming face to face with the monumental wisdom of the legendary Master Kung (better known by his Latinized name of Confucius) and others has been an experience both revealing and at the same time very humbling.

The Master's influence is to be found in the greater part of all proverbs that emanate from China.

Confucius encouraged a careful study of the outside world in his followers, as well as a process of deep thought through which they came to consider and judge their observations. His ideal was to achieve human perfection, and he wanted his followers to develop the facility needed to judge matters skillfully, rather than to simply learn a set of rules and live by them.

It is my sincere hope that a perusal of these pages will help the reader embrace a wider perspective in life and see things in a slightly different light. If we can absorb just a little of the profound wisdom of the Orient, we will be better equipped to interpret the world around us.

Confucius' Golden Rule was: "Never impose upon others what you would not choose for yourself." I happily impose this collection on my esteemed readers.

I thank David Potter for the help he offered me with some translations.

—GERD DE LEY

A note to the readers: The quotes presented in these pages comes in the form of proverbs and aphorisms—i.e., common sayings and generational wisdom for which there is no direct attribution possible. As such, these quotes are presented as they should be received: as standalone pieces of time-honored wisdom.

On
Animals

Once bitten by an adder, you will never walk through the high grass again.

Better to be a free bird on the roof than a wealthy concubine in the house.

Do not be a savage bull on the outside and a shy mouse on the inside.

To feed the ambition in your heart is like carrying a tiger under your arm.

An ant may well destroy a whole dam.

An ape is an ape, a varlet is a varlet,
though they be clad in silk or scarlet.

All asses wag their ears.

The avarice of a man is like a snake trying to swallow an elephant.

Hear the pig's cries at the butcher's at midnight, and you know what the battlefield is like.

Blowing up a bear with dynamite brings no meat to the hunter.

A good bee never lands on a fallen flower.

A bird does not sing because he has the answer to something, he sings because he has a song.

A singing bird killed furnishes no flesh.

Clumsy birds better take off a little earlier.

Border guards are food for the wolves and tigers.

A large bull cannot pick his own lice.

If you agree to carry the calf, they'll make you carry the cow.

You do not satisfy a camel by giving him a little porridge on a spoon.

Care killed the cat.

When the cat has gone, the rats come out to stretch themselves.

What the caterpillar calls the end, the rest of the world calls a butterfly.

It is difficult to catch a black cat in a dark room, especially when it is not there.

All cats love fish but fear to wet their paws.

When a centipede dies on the wall it does not fall down.

Charity is not a bone you throw to a dog, but a bone you share with a dog.

An overcrowded chicken farm produces fewer eggs.

Men who like wild pheasants often despise the chicken from their own farmyard.

Better be the head of a chicken than the tail of a cow.

Cicadas invent a thousand tunes without tiring.

Do not play a flute before a cow.

The daughter of a crab does not give birth to a bird.

No one believes a crow bearing good news.

The black dog gets the food; the white dog gets the blame.

Dogs have so many friends because they wag their tails, not their tongues.

He who plays the donkey must not be surprised that he gets everyone on his back.

Donkey's lips do not fit onto a horse's mouth.

He who wants to be a dragon must eat many little snakes.

The roast duck can fly no more.

When the dust is clear, one knows if he is riding a horse or an ass.

One earthworm can catch ten eels.

Even a big elephant can be caught in one female hair.

Elephant tusks cannot grow out of a dog's mouth.

Exaggeration is to paint a snake and add legs.

A fly before his own eye is bigger than an elephant in the next field.

Don't let the falcon loose until you see the hare.

Give a man a fish and you feed him for a day. Teach a man to fish and you feed him for a lifetime.

If you are not a fish, how can you know if the fish are happy?

Looking for fish? Don't climb a tree.

A dried fish cannot be used as a cat's pillow.

Better a fox's fur than the skins of a thousand sheep.

You can't catch two frogs with one hand.

With a frog in the well, you don't talk about the ocean.

Do not mistake a goat's beard for a fine stallion's tail.

God tempers the wind to the shorn lamb.

All his geese are swans.

The hare does not eat the grass around his burrow.

A person whose heart is not content is like a snake which tries to swallow an elephant.

When the hen crows in the morning, the family is doomed.

Four horses cannot overtake the tongue.

The hinge of a door is never crowded with insects.

You shouldn't give fish to a hungry man, you should teach him how to fish.

If you are hunting for a red deer, then ignore the hares.

Don't stand by a tree stump waiting for a hare.

The horse's reins do not fit an ass.

The Koreans hunt the tiger during one half of the year, while the tiger hunts the Koreans during the other half.

The lotus springs from the mud.

He who is covered in lice doesn't scratch himself
any more.

The mantis seizes the locust but does not see the
yellow bird behind him.

With money, a dragon; without it, a worm.

Monkey see, monkey do.

Even the meanest wolf will not devour its own mother.

Go and sit on the mountain top to see how tigers fight.

If a mouse is hungry enough, it will jump down the cat's throat.

Do not burn your house to get rid of the mouse.

Give the mule a beating and the horse will also be afraid.

A nod is as good as a wink to a blind horse.

The former nun is more poisonous than a snake.

There are many oxen that do not survive too many visits to the veterinary surgeon.

Whilst wrangling over a quarter of pig, you can lose a flock of sheep.

If a man becomes powerful, even his chicken and his dog go to heaven.

When the rabbit is dead, the hunting-dog is next on the menu.

A rat who gnaws at a cat's tail invites destruction.

When you aim at the rat, beware of the vase.

You must have crossed the river before you may tell the crocodile he has bad breath.

Even the sheep with a tiger's skin trembles when the wolf is nearby.

The silent duck gets the worm.

Those who wear the silk don't rear the worms.

When a snail slobbers, don't ask why.

The snake says: "The road is winding, not I."

It is difficult for a snake to go back to hell once he has tasted heaven.

A dead songbird gives us a sad meal.

A sparrow may be small, but it has everything it needs.

A strong steed cannot be raised in the yard.

Don't draw a sword against a louse.

How can the swallow understand the aspirations
of the swan?

Even a tiger takes a nap from time to time.

The tiger pretends to be a vegetarian.

Do not try to escape a flood by grabbing the tail
of a tiger.

Do not shave the head of a tiger with the tail of a snake.

A tiger does not take insults from sheep.

Tiger, leopard, dog and sheep. They all look the same without their hair.

Silly toad: planning a meal of goose!

A weasel comes to say "Happy New Year" to the chickens.

Better the cold blast of winter than the hot breath of a pursuing elephant.

If wishes were horses, beggars would ride.

Some wolves try to be a tiger.

There are those who burn the entire wood just to chase away the wolves.

When a youth takes the scorpion for a bed-fellow, the aged go out on the roof.

On Beauty

Abroad we judge the dress; at home we judge the man.

Don't pick withered blossoms on your way when you have a plum-flower at home.

Take care of your own gate, and do not think of other men's wives.

Beauty is potent but money is omnipotent.

The woman who tells her age is either too young to have anything to lose or too old to have anything to gain.

A man cannot be known by his looks, nor can the sea be measured with a bushel basket.

Not every bald head belongs to a monk.

Too many colors can be blinding; too many sounds can deafen, and too many tastes can ruin the palate.

Beauty without virtue is like a flower with no fragrance.

The bigger the compliments, the smaller the tenderness.

Covetousness bursts the sack.

The worst cracks are to be found in the most beautiful vases.

The family of elegant daughters are the worst thieves.

No wise man takes responsibility for an eighteen year old daughter.

Better a diamond with a flaw than a pebble without.

When the ear will not listen, the heart escapes sorrow.

What the eyes do not see, the heart does not feel.

When fate smiles at us, we meet friends; when fate is against us, we meet a beautiful woman.

A girl of eighteen looks like a flower.

A girl that blushes too much, knows too much.

A great lover is not one who romances a different women every night.
A great lover is one who romances the same woman for a lifetime.

Long hair, short ideas.

Idleness breeds lust.

Better a broken piece of jade than a tile that is intact.

The less kings and beautiful women speak, the more they say.

Kissing is like drinking salted water: you drink, and your thirst increases.

Love is an eye that doesn't see anything.

An ugly man takes a beautiful woman to be his wife.

Nine out of ten matchmakers are liars.

When a finger is pointing at the moon, the fool looks at the finger.

Music pleases the heart and warms the mind.

Men love their own compositions and other men's wives.

New things always smell good.

An obscure style is a blind mirror.

If you have nothing else to offer me, offer me your smile.

Do not tremble at the thought of being old and weak; tremble because your heart gets cold though you are still young.

A divided orange tastes just as good.

Passion too deep seems like none.

The strongest perfumes attract the ugliest flies.

A person is three parts real and seven parts artificial—beauty needs some help.

Poverty and ugliness are difficult to hide.

Prostitutes are willows along the road, flowers on a wall.

A rose has no back.

A ruby can be covered in mud but that does not make it dirty.

When you are well dressed, you don't mind that your shadow is behind you.

Whilst her lips say, "Enough", her eyes shout for more.

The pen of the tongue should be dipped in the ink of the heart.

A bright light in a dark tunnel is brighter than all the lights in a seven-story temple.

Even ugly faces are worth looking at, and that is a great comfort for most people.

Without a bright mirror, a woman cannot know if the powder is smooth on her face.

A woman can live the life of a prisoner. She can live the life of a princess. Or she can be herself.

When a chaste woman desires pleasure, she gets it properly.

It's not the beauty of a woman that blinds the man; the man blinds himself.

A pretty woman at home is the enemy of all the ugly ones.

A woman's beauty makes fish sink and wild geese fall from the sky.

Small is beautiful.

What is lighter than a feather? The wind!
Lighter than the wind? The spirit!
Lighter than the spirit? The woman!
Lighter than the woman? Nothing at all!

On Experience

A good advice may sound terrible but will be good for you just as a good medicine may taste bitter but will be good for your health.

He who will not accept an old man's advice will someday be a beggar.

Unpalatable advice benefits conduct.

Good advice is beyond price.

Chi Wen Tzu always thought three times before taking action. Twice would have been quite enough.

Better to eat a single good pear than a basket of rotten ones.

Hear all sides and you will be enlightened. Hear one side, and you will be in the dark.

In a narrow lane, watch out for a dagger.

Don't lift off the lid too soon.

Be sincere and true to your word, serious and careful in your actions; and you will get along even among barbarians.

If one man guards a narrow pass, ten thousand cannot get through.

He who treads softly goes far.

When you meet someone better than yourself, turn your thoughts to becoming his equal.

You can plug one person's ears, but you can't close everyone's eyes.

Use the days of plenty to think of days of nothing.

If you plan for a year, plant rice.
If you plan for ten years, plant trees.
If you plan for one hundred years, educate your children.

Though his hair is white, he is as young as ever.

To ask is not a crime. To be rejected is not a calamity.

What you cannot avoid, welcome.

A bad man talks about what he has eaten and drunk, a good man about what he has seen and heard.

A stroke of bad luck is merely an opportunity with a mask on.

The beginning and the end reach out their hands to each other.

The benevolent see benevolence, and the wise see wisdom.

Bitterness is lurking behind each joy.

The blind are quick at hearing; the deaf are quick at sight.

Every book must be chewed to get out its juice.

If you have an itchy foot, it is no use scratching the outside of your boot.

Borrowed money shortens time; working for others lengthens it.

A full bottle makes no sound; a half-full bottle sloshes around.

While the boy is small, you can see the man.

A buckle is a great addition to an old shoe.

He who is without cash in his pocket might as well be buried in a rice tub with his mouth sewed up.

Only chaos is always pressed for time.

Cheap things are not good, good things are not cheap.

The first time you cheat me, be ashamed.

The second time, it is I who must be ashamed.

He who can handle a writing brush will never have to beg.

A cold man can't be choosy about clothes.

Coming events cast their shadows before them.

When a conversation turns nasty, to say one word more is a waste of breath.

Whenever two people go to court, one gets rich—the third!

Debts no longer keeps a man awake when he is full of it.

Know deeply the depths and the details.

He who has lavish desires will spend extravagantly.

You must despise yourself before the others do.

Those whose ways are different can't lay plans for one another.

When a disease relapses, there is no cure.

All things depart from that which is different from themselves, and follow that which is the same.

Be careful of your dreams, they may come true.

Three times an early rise makes a whole day.

Economize now or suffer want later.

The proper man understands equity, the small man profits.

Examinations are a deadly struggle in the thorny enclosure.

Experience is a comb which nature gives us when we are bald.

If you have never been fooled, you'll never become an expert.

Deal with the faults of others as gently as with your own.

He that fights and runs away
may live to fight another day.

Do not dress in clothes made of leaves when going to put out a fire.

Forewarned is forearmed.

Fortune knocks but thrice.

The depth of the foundation determines the height of the wall.

Hire a young roof-worker, but consult an old doctor.

Real gold is not afraid of the melting pot.

Good luck beats early rising.

Greed is always hungry.

Guilt is always jealous.

When men speak of the future, the gods laugh.

The happiness is in your pocket; don't spend it all.

Health is not valued until illness comes.

If you do not go up the hill, you cannot see the plain.

We must always have old memories and young hopes.

A maker of idols is never an idolater.

After the long slumber of ignorance, a single word can change a man forever.

When you are ill for long enough, you become a skilled physician.

Impatient people talk too much.

Burn the right incense in the right temple.

Insults often cover up a weak case.

You inherit intelligence, wisdom must be learned.

Tell me and I'll forget; show me and I may remember; involve me and I'll understand.

The jail is closed day and night and always full;
temples are always open and still empty.

One key does not rattle.

Laughter is the medicine to cure one hundred
illnesses.

Win your lawsuit and lose your money.

Learning is a treasure no thief can touch.

The longer the explanation, the bigger the lie.

If luck is against you, even water will stick in your teeth.

If you do without something for long enough, then you don't need it.

Elderly people say that every new year is worse than the one before.

Some people are already old when they are three.

Opportunities multiply as they are seized.

He who knows about others may be learned, but he who understands himself is more intelligent.

Pain is easier to endure than an itch.

The past remembered is a good guide for the future.

An ounce of practice is worth a pound of theory.

Your reputation is your second life.

Rice obtained by crookedness will not boil up into good food.

It is hard to be right all the time, but it is easy to be wrong sometimes.

Rivalry between scholars improves science.

Excessive scoldings and beatings lose their intended effect.

Shame is forgotten, debts are not.

I was angered, for I had no shoes.

Then I met a man who had no feet.

Even a skilled hand can't sew two needles at the same time.

He who does not regularly put on clean socks will never get used to circus life.

To the sophisticated person, there's nothing new under the sun.

If you don't speculate, you can't accumulate.

Too much spirit shows a lack of it.

The spirit never perishes, only the body decays.

However strong you are, there is always someone stronger.

If you wish to succeed, consult three old people.

The superior man is slow in his words and earnest in his conduct.

You will not develop a talent unless you give it a chance.

Reviewing the old and deducing the new makes a teacher.

The able doctor acts before sickness comes.

Be thrifty in good times to survive in bad times.

Two of a trade can never agree.

To fell the tree very quickly, you must sharpen the axe twice.

It is easy to court trouble, but hard to avert it.

A walk after a meal makes for a long life.

Water drowns a good swimmer more often than a bad one.

You cannot appreciate the weight until you shoulder the load.

Wise is he who listens to his body.

Wise people are not always learned; learned people are not always wise.

The wise man, although he keeps in the background, stays ahead.

A wise man is always good but a good man is not always wise.

The wise man learns more from his enemies than a fool does from his friends.

May you live in interesting times.

The wise man and the tortoise travel but never leave their home.

May your life be filled with experiences.

You need your wits about you the most when you are dealing with an idiot.

A patient woman can roast an ox with a lantern.

Square words won't fit into a round ear.

His mouth still smells of mother's milk.

You are not as young as you were but nowhere near as old as you hope to become.

On
Family and
the Home

Beat your drum inside the house to spare the neighbors.

If you keep showing off, your family budget will go down the hill.

You've got to do your own growing, no matter how tall your grandfather is.

No sex till a hundred days after giving birth for those who want to live long and happy with their wives.

To forget one's ancestors is to be a brook without a source, a tree without a root.

Benevolence is a house full of peace.

An old bachelor compares life with a shirt button that hangs often by a thread.

When the baby does not cry, the breast does not swell.

Birth is much, but breeding is more.

It is too late to pierce the bride's ears when she is already sitting in the wedding chair.

Brothers are like hands and feet.

Even the worst brother is still a brother; the best spouse is not even a blood relative.

Keeping your chastity is not as good as remarrying.

Even if a woman gives birth to nine children, each child is different.

A small cottage wherein laughter lives is worth more than a castle full of tears.

It is easier to rule a country than to rule your wife.

A couple that has one happy day together is blessed with a hundred days of tenderness.

An unmarried daughter is like a sack of rice on which tax is not yet paid.

When there are too many daughters-in-law; the kettle never gets cleaned.

When a family runs into trouble, the oldest daughterinlaw grows a beard.

If you want dinner, don't insult the cook.

Divorce is a double edged sword; you can hurt yourself when you make the cut.

Discipline springs from love.

The best kind of closed door is the one you can leave unlocked.

If thine enemy wrong thee, buy each of his children a drum.

The family house home is a territory for the boys and a restaurant for girls.

Every family has a book that is read with shame.

One family builds a wall, two families enjoy it.

Govern a family as you would cook a small fish—very gently.

The father who does not teach his son his duties is equally guilty with the son who neglects them.

A father cannot hide from his children if he is an ox or a horse.

The older the fiddle, the sweeter the tune.

Before the door, your footprints are overgrown with moss.

A friend, one soul, two bodies.

It is easier to govern a country than a son.

Grandfather built the street in which father drives his car.

The house with an old grandparent harbors a jewel.

One guest does not need two hosts.

Whoever buys a house must examine the beams; whoever wants a wife must look at her mother.

To move into a new house means three years of poverty.

The ugly housewife is a treasure at home.

Don't lie to your friends, and don't tell the truth to your husband.

Even the best judge cannot settle a domestic dispute.

When her son-in-law has ulcers, the mother-in-law goes on a diet.

A man thinks he knows, but a woman knows better.

Man is the head of the family, woman the neck that turns the head.

A quarrel between man and wife is like cutting water with a sword.

A young man must marry when he is young, an old one when he is old.

Good parents, happy marriages; good children, fine funerals.

The perfect marriage is like the blossom of flowers by a full moon.

You can drop your father, even if he is a judge, but you can't drop your mother, even if she is a beggar.

Call her "mother" once and she will become your mother forever.

Love me little, love me long.

If you want to play, go to your grandmother's house; if you are looking for trouble, go to your mother-in-law's.

If you want a favor from your husband's mother, flatter first her youngest sister.

It cannot rain at your neighbor's place without you getting your feet wet.

When your neighbor walks through your orchard, the polite thing to do is to ignore it.

There are no filial children at the bedside of chronically ill parents.

All people are your relatives, therefore expect only trouble from them.

When the man stays potent, the family is happy.

Public before private, and country before family.

Reunion after a brief separation is better than a honeymoon.

Parents cherish their youngest son, grandparents their oldest grandson.

The son must bury his father, the father must marry his son.

You are more intimate with your grandson than with your son.

A son with grey hair can still be beaten by his father, but not the married daughter.

It is a sad situation for a son-in-law when his mother-in-law praises him.

There is a black sow in every household.

Spouses that love each other say a thousand things without speaking.

He who teaches me for one day is my father for life.

A girl can't drink tea from two families.

The hardest step is over the threshold.

There's always an ear on the other side of the wall, and there's bound to be someone outside the window.

At the border many strong men,
Back at home, many widows.

Water is wine for those in love.

The girl will have little fortune if she doesn't cry on her wedding ceremony.

If your children are wicked, they don't deserve to inherit; if they are good and hard working, they don't need to.

A widow is a boat without a rudder.

She who is the wife of one man cannot eat the rice of two.

It takes a hundred soldiers to make a camp, but only one wife to make a home.

Do not curse your wife after sundown, unless you want to sleep alone.

Without wine in the bottle, it is hard to have guests.

On Friendship

True friendship is clear like water.
False friendship is sweet, like honey.

The more acquaintances you have, the less you know them.

Don't go on a man's bond in public, nor guarantee his debts in private.

Behave to everyone as if you were receiving a great guest.

As soon as two people agree, yellow mud becomes into pure gold.

Alms given openly will be rewarded in secret.

An answer that does not resolve a quarrel, makes a thousand new ones.

Mutual assistance makes mutual success.

Blame yourself as you would blame others; excuse others as you would excuse yourself.

Ceremony is the smoke of friendship.

Men, not walls, make a city.

A courtesy much entreated is half recompensed.

To stop drinking, study a drunkard when you are sober.

To have emotions without intelligence is a misery; to have intelligence without emotions is a barren desert.

He who cannot agree with his enemies is controlled by them.

The delicacy of the feast is the learned guest.

He who flatters me is my enemy, who blames me is my teacher.

Quarrel with a friend—and you are both wrong.

He who abuses you to your face, can still be a friend.

When men are friendly, the water is sweet.

Gifts reflect those who give them.

He who allows himself to be given away is not worth being accepted again.

Happiness is someone to love, something to do, and something to hope for.

People who are late are often happier than those who have to wait for them.

Love is blind, friendship closes its eyes.

An accidental meeting is more pleasant than a planned one.

The best under us are like oil-lamps: they throw light on the others, not on themselves.

A broken relation is hard to put back together.

The scent of a rose will always stay on the hand of the giver.

Long and short match each other.

First time strangers, second time friends.

Better to drink the weak tea of a friend than the sweet wine of an enemy.

When a man gets to the top, his friends and relatives accompany him.

When someone gives you a drop of water, reward him with a never ending source.

On Labor

Behind an able man there are always other able men.

People remember the leopard by its spots.
People remember a person by his accomplishments.

Taking action without doing anything makes a lot of rules superfluous.

You cannot propel yourself forward by patting yourself on the back.

To go beyond is as bad as to fall short.

Clean out the drainpipes while the weather is good.

Make something big by starting with it when small.

It takes little effort to watch a man carry a load.

You must chop before you can plane and cut before you can polish.

One cannot manage too many affairs: like pumpkins in the water, one pops up while you try to hold down the other.

Steady application makes a superior product.

Troops are valued for their quality, not for their quantity.

A full bag is heavy to carry, but an empty one is heavier.

You can't fill your belly painting pictures of bread.

No matter how big, one beam cannot support a house.

Best is often the enemy of the good.

A blind man can see his mouth.

One hundred bodies cannot make good a broken leg.

An old broom knows the dirty corners best.

He who carves the Buddha never worships him.

You have only just immersed one calabash and another one quickly appears.

A butcher becomes a Buddha the moment he drops his cleaver.

A high building, a low foundation.

Locks cannot be made from good iron, soldiers are not made out of good people.

The capable are assigned more tasks.

If one remains as careful at the end as one was at the beginning, there will be no failure.

A project that you built for a long time can be destroyed in one careless moment.

For everything there is a cause.

Mallet strikes chisel; chisel splits wood.

Whoever tears his clothes must mend them himself.

A cloth is not woven with one thread only.

There is no one to sweep a common hall.

One who has time to complain has time to submit patches.

A craftsman who wants to be rich makes carts and coffins.

Large demands on oneself and little demands on others keep resentment at bay.

Diligence without frugality is like a needle without thread.

Endure the most, become the best.

Constant effort yields certain success.

He who always eats the roots of a plant is capable of anything.

The first thing to do is to start and the second is to continue.

Many a good face is under a ragged hat.

To give up halfway through is to fail completely.

A single fiber does not make a thread.

Be first in the field, the last to the couch.

Great things can be reduced to small things, and small things can be reduced to nothing.

One generation builds the street on which the next will walk.

Other men are the carving knife and serving dish; we are the fish and the meat.

Your goal is just around the corner.

The best things in life are free.

Look beneath the Great Wall, and you will see bones upon bones of dead men.

Haste inevitably leads to ignorance.

When you hate somebody, advise him to build a house.

The best place to find helping hands is at the end of your own arms.

The darkest hour is that before the dawn.

To have saved one human life is worth more than to build a pagoda with seven stores.

Insanity is doing the same thing in the same way and expecting a different outcome.

Inspiration comes only after perspiration.

Choose a job you love, and you will never have to work a day in your life.

Lazy people always want to do everything at the same time.

He who has his legs spread out, won't be able to march forward.

The load carried by another doesn't seem very heavy.

A good calculator does not need artificial aids.

If you behave like a machine you will have the heart of a machine.

To overshoot the mark is as bad as not reaching your goal.

No mill, no meal.

Misery acquaints men with strange bedfellows.

One monk shoulders water by himself; two can still share the labor among them. When it comes to three, they have to go thirsty.

He who wants to make a mountain, must start with digging a hole.

When a nation is filled with strife, then do patriots flourish.

All gardeners know better than other gardeners.

The more you sweat in Peacetime, the less you bleed during War.

You can learn more about a person in one hour of play than you can in one year of work.

To know precisely when to start the ploughing is better than having the best plough.

The pole is easy to carry if the load is balanced.

Little posts cannot support heavy weights.

The little pot is soonest hot.

Put up or shut up.

Never do anything standing that you can do sitting, or anything sitting that you can do lying down.

Separately we are grains of sand, together we are a gold nugget.

One sings, all follow.

Talking doesn't get your rice cooked.

Even when sandwiches rain from the sky, you will still have to stoop to pick them up.

Sow early and you will reap early.

Work, and you will be strong; sit, and you will stink.

You have to study to learn to be good.

Success is three parts genius and seven parts hard work.

No sweet without sweat.

Those without talents are poor. Those without ambition are weak.

Unity can turn dirt into gold.

Without the fire of enthusiasm there is no warmth in victory.

It is easy to watch but difficult to do.

Dig the well before you are thirsty.

A work ill done must be done twice.

The day of the storm is not the time for thatching.

A thousand workers, a thousand plans.

On Leadership

Adversity is a mirror that shows the real character of a man.

The person who says it cannot be done should not interrupt the person doing it.

When one person does a bad deed, one thousand people suffer.

Instead of being concerned that you are not known, see to the worthy of being known.

An army burning with righteous indignation is bound to win.

Arrogance is the enemy of victory.

Be gentle and you can be bold; be frugal and you can be liberal; avoid putting yourself before others and you can become a leader among men.

Benevolence brings honor; cruelty, disgrace.

A bow that has been stretched too much loses its tension.

If you bow at all, bow low.

You must empty a box before you fill it again.

Business must be dealt with promptly, just as food must be eaten hot.

He who does not know what to do in his spare time is not a businessman.

Calamity is man's true touchstone.

The overturned cart up ahead serves as a warning to the carts behind.

Easy to keep the castle that was never besieged.

A just cause will enjoy abundant support, while an unjust cause will find little support.

Claiming certainty without corroborating evidence is stupid.

Only the wisest and the stupidest of men never change.

Two leaps per chasm is fatal.

The surest way to get cheated is to believe you are smarter than the others.

If one piece is moved wrongly, the whole game is lost.

A good client doesn't change shop in three years, a good shop doesn't change clients in three years.

Three foolish cobblers with their wits combined equal a master mind.

If you can command yourself, you can command the world.

The greatest conqueror wins without struggle.

The conquerors are kings; the defeated are bandits.

Kill one to warn a hundred.

Corporations have neither bodies to be punished nor souls to be damned.

When those in authority are corrupt, everybody tends to follow suit.

A crisis is an opportunity riding the dangerous wind.

The collapse of a dam can begin with just antholes.

A good drum does not have to be beaten hard.

If you are prepared for difficulties, they won't come.

He who cannot suffer discomfort will not be called for important things.

Distinguished persons are apt to be forgetful.

When the deal is done, discuss it no more; it is difficult to collect dispersed water.

When with dwarfs, do not talk about pygmies.

Rare is the executive who can weigh the faults of his colleagues without putting his thumb on the scale.

When the flight is not high the fall is not heavy.

Enough feathers can sink a boat.

Do not bring firewood to put a fire out.

He who could foresee affairs three days in advance would be rich for a thousand years.

A great fortune depends on luck, a small one on diligence.

A great general does not need to blow his own trumpet.

You can't clap with one hand.

A great man is hard on himself. A small man is hard on others.

Our greatest glory is not in never failing, but in rising every time we fail.

Happiness without intellect is a sack full of holes.

Honesty is the only currency with which you can pay everywhere.

An honest magistrate cannot succeed.

An honorable man is a majority of one.

The problem with idiots is that they only find things stupid when they are not.

A good intermediary must always be able to lie a little.

He who is in control of himself can rule the world.

When a king makes a mistake, all the people suffer.

The law is good, but people are not.

The more laws made, the more criminals created.

When the effective leader is finished with his work, the people say it happened naturally.

A leader is best when people hardly know he exists.

To lead the people, walk behind them.

A man is worth more than what he is paid.

The most successful manager leads without dictating.

He who is master of himself cannot tolerate another boss.

Masters are made, not born.

He who is always mild-mannered is invincible.

The wrath of the mob is difficult to oppose.

The best tacticians are never impulsive and the best leaders are never arrogant.

The good mouth doesn't curse and the good hand doesn't fight.

Cut off your nose to spite your face.

Pirates that attack each other seldom do good business.

Nothing brings greater misfortune than killing those who have already surrendered.

Pride goes before and shame follows after.

With more problems, a nation becomes united.

The sage manages affairs without action and spreads doctrines without words.

You always win by not saying the things you don't have to say.

Do not employ handsome servants.

Ugly women and dumb maidservants are of invaluable worth.

When there are seven navigators for eight seamen, the ship will sink.

Three humble shoemakers brainstorming equal one great statesman.

He who cannot laugh should not open a shop.

It is easy to get a thousand soldiers, but difficult to get one general.

Of all the stratagems, to know when to quit is the best.

Powerful people often suffer from amnesia.

If you suspect a man, don't employ him, and if you employ him, don't suspect him.

Do not expose money to eyes.

Those who are prospering do not argue about taxes.

One teapot can serve five teacups, but seldom do you see one teacup serving five teapots.

He who defines the terms wins the argument.

When three of us are together, there is certainly a master for me among them.

The timid can't become generals.

One measures the towers by their shadows and great people by those who envy them.

The true man will not compromise his principles for a meager reward.

He who is sure of his victory will not start a war.

To use violence is to already be defeated.

All is fair in war.

He who can follow his own will is a king.

On
Life and Death

Better die ten years early than live ten years poor.

To die is to stop living but to stop living is something entirely different than dying.

Do not count the things you lost, but the things you still have.

When mourning gives full expression to grief, nothing more can be required.

The last to board is the first to debark.

The higher the climb, the further the fall.

Always look for the coffin at the back of your carriage.

The court official in one life has seven rebirths as a beggar.

When you are dead, your fists are empty.

At birth we bring nothing, at death we take away nothing.

Look upon death as a going home.

Often one finds one's destiny just where one hides to avoid it.

To complete a thing, a hundred years is not sufficient; to destroy it, one day is more than enough.

The devil never grants long leases.

Make sure you leave some fat for the other side.

It's better to die two years early than to live one year too long.

When the butcher dies, do you think we shall eat our pork with the bristles on?

Back to the draught is face to the grave.

One cannot refuse to eat just because there is a chance of being choked.

Emperor Ts'ong-tchen lived for eight hundred and eighty years but still not long enough to see black coal turned white.

Fat fries and burns itself.

Dream of a funeral and you hear of a marriage.

All the past died yesterday; the future is born today.

A general's triumph means ten thousand rotting bones.

The more you are afraid of ghosts, the more ghosts you see.

Heaven is only three feet above your head.

Heaven lent you a soul
Earth will lend a grave.

There are no fans in hell.

Do not judge someone before his coffin is closed.

You will never be punished for making people die of laughter.

Life begins at seventy.

Life is but a smile on the lips of death.

Life is a tragedy for those who feel and a comedy for those who think.

Man fools himself. He prays for a long life and he fears old age.

Outside noisy, inside empty.

Paper and brush may kill a man; you don't need a knife.

Fight poison with poison.

Only two gentlemen are very busy in this world: mister Profit and mister Glory.

That which is quickly acquired is easily lost.

He who seeks revenge should remember to dig two graves.

To avoid sickness, eat less; to prolong life, worry less.

He who swims in sin shall sink in sorrow.

Some smiles hide a knife.

You cannot prevent the birds of sorrow from flying over your head, but you can prevent them from building nests in your hair.

Shed no tear until you see your own coffin.

Thirst is never quenched by drinking poison.

If you want to weaken something, make it first very strong.

Every kind of wood is grey when they are reduced to ashes.

Better to drink one cup of tea in this world than to eat a plate of rice in the next.

Worry causes aging.

The Yangtse never runs backwards; man recaptures not his youth.

Yesterday did not stay.

A young branch takes on all the bends that one gives it.

On Nature

Dig a ditch while the sky is clear, or you'll have a flood when it rains.

Don't pull on the plant shoots to help them grow.

The best time to plant a tree was 20 years ago. The second best time is today.

When eating bamboo sprouts, remember the man who planted them.

Our body is the Universe in miniature.

A slanted branch has a slanted shadow.

The butterfly only visits beautiful flowers.

Floating clouds have no place to rest.

Just because men do not like the cold, Heaven will not stop the winter.

The corn is not choked by the weeds but by the negligence of the farmer.

The day did not know that night had fallen.

There is no dew that does not wet your shoes.

Follow what is natural and you will last longer; disregard what is natural and it will be a disaster.

He who cheats the earth will be cheated by the earth.

The evening crowns the days.

No matter how clever the farmer is, he will never grow sunflowers without seed.

The farmer hopes for rain, the walker hopes for sunshine, and the gods hesitate.

The flower in your garden is less beautiful than the wild one.

The peony is large, but useless to man; the jujube blossom, though small, ripens into precious fruit.

Pick the flower when it is ready to be picked.

As long as there are forests, one need not worry about firewood.

Ripe fruit falls by itself, but it does not fall into your mouth.

Life begins the day you start a garden.

If you do not fear the gods, just listen to the thunder.

If I keep a green bough in my heart, the singing bird will come.

The green of grass as seen afar is gone when near.

An old man in love is like a flower in winter.

There was a man from Sung who pulled at his rice plants because he was worried about their failure to grow.

The harvest of a whole year depends on what you sow in the springtime.

Ice three feet thick is not frozen in a day.

He who shakes trees only in winter will die from hunger.

One small grain is the treasure of treasures.

One bite of the peach of immortality is worth more than a basket full of apricots.

You can bend a sapling as far as you can pull it.

If you cannot be a shining star in the sky then be a lantern in your house.

Falling leaves return to their roots.

Even the most beautiful morning cannot bring back the evening.

He who stands still in the mud sticks in it.

In nature there are neither rewards or punishments; there are consequences.

An oak is not felled at one stroke.

Even oceans may at last run dry.

Sit quietly, doing nothing; spring comes, and the grass grows by itself.

The stars make no noise.

Patience is like a tree that has bitter roots, but gives sweet fruit.

Nature, time and patience are the three great physicians.

The stronger the thunder, the weaker the rain.

If rain bothers you, you can always jump into the sea.

One hundred rivers return to the sea.

A great river is the result of many little drops.

When the lamps in the house are lit it is like the flowering of lotus on the lake.

Slander cannot make a good man bad: when the flood recedes, the rock is there.

When all is red and purple, spring is surely due.

Spring is sooner recognized by plants than by men.

From the most ordinary of oysters often comes the finest pearls.

You can't expect both ends of a sugar cane are as sweet.

It is not necessary to light a candle to the sun.

The sun has risen twice today.

The swing of a sword can't cut the mist from the sky.

If you want good tea, then first look for good water.

Use one thorn to extract another.

A thunderclap surpasses all noises.

You can't buy an inch of time with an inch of gold.

The tide must ebb before it flows.

The most beautiful tomorrow cannot bring yesterday back for us.

A tree that can't be spanned by one man, grows from a minuscule seed.

When the tree falls, the shadow flies.

After shaking a tree, shake again. It costs nothing.

Water that has reached its level does not flow.

When the water falls, the stone becomes visible.

The purer the water, the less fish.

The world is our house. Keep it clean.

There is no wall through which the wind cannot pass.

Open the window and improve your health.

Heaven doesn't cancel winter because men dislike cold.

May it always be spring with you.

On Knowing Oneself

It is not the failure of others to appreciate your abilities which should trouble you, but rather their failure to appreciate theirs.

The mind is the lord of man's body.

Be the best of all the things you want to be.

Man becomes the master of difficult situations by refusing the assistance of weak men.

If you stuff your mouth full, you can't chew thoroughly.

Recognize that you know what you know, and that you are ignorant of what you do not know.

You cannot undo a stupid act by reproaching yourself.

Control your emotion or it will control you.

Anger is always more harmful than the insult that caused it.

A man without a favorite author is lost. For the rest of his life he will be forever like an unfertilized egg.

It is normal to be average.

After being struck on the head by an axe, it is a positive pleasure to be beaten about the body with a wooden club.

What shall one lean on if one has no backbone?

As long as you have one little hair on your head, you are not bald.

You own many houses and hotels, you only sleep in one bed.

If one's aim is wealth one cannot be beneficent; if one's aim is benevolence one cannot be worthy.

A fool in a hurry drinks tea with a fork.

Copy three times a medicine-book and you are ill for the rest of your life.

He who knows his boundaries will always be able to impose the necessary limitations upon himself.

It is better to light a candle than to curse the darkness.

Don't hang your conscience on your back.

Compromise is only ever a temporary success.

You cannot take white cloth out of a tub full of indigo.

The contented person can never be ruined.

Only a coward knows what his duty is without doing it.

To be able to curse once a day improves happiness and lengthens life.

A defeat becomes a bitter drink when one decides to swallow it.

To pretend to satisfy one's desires with worldly goods is like using straw to put out a fire.

A dictionary can only be read when it is printed.

Those who break down the dikes will themselves be drowned in the inundation.

I hear and I forget.
I see and I remember.
I do and I understand.

Education that only entered your eyes and your ears is like a meal you ate in your dream.

The elbow bends inward.

Envy shoots at others and wounds itself.

What the eyes do not see, the heart does not feel.

The man who wakes up and finds himself famous hasn't been asleep.

There is no greater illusion than fear.

Whoever can see through all fear
will always be safe.

Even the ten fingers cannot be of equal length.

Healthy food cures better than medicine.

Blame yourself as you would blame others; excuse others as you would excuse yourself.

A man who knows that he is a fool is not a great fool.

He who asks a question may be a fool for five minutes; he who asks no questions stays a fool forever.

Better the foot slip than the tongue trip.

Genius can be recognized by its childish simplicity.

A fool cannot forgive; he who can forgive is not a fool.

There are no winners among habitual gamblers.

The careful foot can walk anywhere.

What is a good man?
An example for a bad man.
What is a bad man?
A mirror for a good man.

Govern yourself and you can govern the world.

Governors should not use water for a mirror, but the people.

A day of grief lasts longer than a month of joy.

Those that look for harmony will know where to find it.

Make the hat according to the measurements of your head.

"I heard" is not as good as "I saw."

If Heaven above lets fall a plum, open your mouth.

Who is inferior and is ashamed of it, proves that he really is inferior.

The itch that gives someone skill is difficult to scratch.

If the string is long, the kite flies high.

To know and know that you know, not to know and know that you don't know, *that* is to know.

How do you know what I don't know? You're not me.

Limitations are only borders we create for ourselves.

The height of knowledge is to know nothing.

A man who pats himself on the back risks a broken arm.

A man combs his hair every morning—why not his heart?

'Swallow the medicine but neglect the diet' is ruining the medical science.

Do not be concerned at other men's not knowing you; be concerned at your own want of ability.

Modesty is the companion of success.

One can forgive a murder but not impoliteness.

When you have musk, you will automatically have fragrance.

Who is narrow minded cannot be big hearted.

A man of high principles is someone who can watch a chess game without passing comment.

You can't beat oil out of chaff.

A man can never be perfect in a hundred years; but he may become corrupt in less than a day.

If you must play, decide upon three things at the start: the rules of the game, the stakes, and when to stop.

No needle is sharp at both ends.

Do not let your qualities stand in the way of your progress.

It is better to go hungry with a pure mind than to eat well with an evil one.

Don't promise something when you are full of joy; don't answer letters when you are full of anger.

The quiet and solitary man apprehends the inscrutable.

People are suspicious of the man with a red nose, even if he doesn't drink at all.

He who is satisfied with himself, is rich.

The loss of one night's sleep is followed by ten days of inconvenience.

If you walk on snow, you cannot hide your footprints.

You can only enjoy solitude when you are at peace with yourself.

The one who understands does not speak; the one who speaks does not understand.

He who tiptoes cannot stand; he who strides cannot walk.

He who fills his head instead of his pockets can never be robbed.

What the superior man seeks is in himself. What the mean man seeks is in others.

Who thinks an inch, but talks a yard, needs a kick in the foot.

Don't waste your time thinking about the little things.

Treat thoughts as guests and wishes as children.

Measure your throat before you swallow a bone.

When you cease to strive to understand, then you will know without understanding.

Time is more important than money.

Do not think any vice trivial, and so practice it;
do not think any virtue trivial, and so neglect it.

Virtue practiced to be seen is not real virtue; vice
which fears to be seen is real vice.

Do not tear down the east wall to repair the west.

Weaklings never forgive their enemies.

Overcome one's weaknesses by learning from other's strengths.

May your way always be enlightened by a lucky star.

May your every wish be granted.

May you come to the attention of those in authority.

May you find what you are looking for.

The first decision of a woman is the most intelligent and the last decision most dangerous.

Mistrust yourself before others do.

He who knows much about others may be learned, but he who understands himself is more intelligent.

Know thyself to know others, for heart beats like heart.

On
Travel

If you want to see farther, you have to go higher.

Raise your sail one foot and you get ten feet of wind.

Follow the local custom when you go to a foreign place.

If you ask for directions rudely, you may end up twenty miles from your destination.

The road to high places begins in low places.

Better go than send.

You won't get lost if you frequently ask for directions.

Every hundred miles you will find different customs.

Among barbarians, act like a barbarian.

Put a beggar on horseback and he'll gallop.

From Nanking to Peking buyers are never as smart as the sellers.

It is easy to take a light carriage on a familiar road.

Where there is a cart ahead there is a track behind.

If we don't change our direction we're likely to end up where we're headed.

An ambassador bears no blame.

It is not the destination that is important, but the journey there.

Deviate an inch, lose a thousand miles.

Real people know that what is far away can also be found nearby.

If you have nowhere else to go, stay where you are.

If at home you receive no visitors, then abroad you will have no host.

He who hurries cannot walk with dignity.

Choose your inn before dark, get back on the road before dawn.

An innkeeper never worries if your appetite is big.

A journey of a thousand miles begins with a single step.

The journey is the reward.

It is better to do a kindness near home than go far to burn incense.

Don't listen to what they say. Go see.

Take a second look; it costs you nothing.

Don't look back when you are walking along the edge of a wall.

If ever you heard people speaking about Peking, then don't go there.

He who walks on two roads at the same time arrives nowhere.

All roads lead to Peking.

No matter how big the sea may be, sometimes two ships meet.

It does not matter how slowly you go so long as you do not stop.

He who steps aside for someone broadens the way.

Light travels like an arrow, and time like a shuttle.

A man grows most tired while standing still.

He who travels in a splendid carriage is greeted by strangers as though he were a relative.

Traveller, there is no road. The road is made as you walk.

Only he that has travelled the road knows where the holes are deep.

When you go for a one day trip, carry food for two days.

Shade and light are different in every valley.

One step at a time is good walking.

Great wealth implies great loss.

After all, the world is but a little place.

On Truth

The true gentleman does not preach what he practices till he has practiced what he preaches.

One never accuses without a little bit of lying.

A great achievement has always ended with a greater failure.

Better be too credulous than too skeptical.

Out of a tangled ball one has to draw a silk thread.

Only when you know why you have hit the target, can you truly say you have learned archery.

To win an argument does not mean you have convinced your opponent.

When no one begs, all are equal.

Believe only thirty percent of what you hear before you believe one hundred percent.

Great boast, small roast.

Never boast; you might meet someone who knew you as a child.

Everyone speaks well of the bridge which carries him over.

Before the beginning of great brilliance, there must be chaos.

True character is revealed in moments of extreme anger.

Clay is molded to make a vessel, but the utility of the vessel lies in the space where there is nothing.

A clean hand wants no washing.

The best way to keep a crime a secret is not to commit it.

The sick devil would like to be a monk.

Every drama requires a fool.

Drunkards talk to the gods.

Though the emperor be rich, he cannot buy one extra year.

Predestined enemies will always meet in a narrow alleyway.

Enough is as good as a feast.

Evil deeds done in secret are seen by the spirits as a flash of fire.

Faith and dishonesty are other words for uselessness.

Fame is empty.

Better dry one tear on the face of a farmer than get a hundred smiles from a minister.

He who hides his faults plans to make more.

The first favor is a favor, the second an obligation.

The flatterer makes you climb up a tree then takes the ladder away.

Enough food and a pipe full of tobacco makes you equal to the immortals.

He who is too funny ceases to be funny.

Ill-gotten gains are like snow that is sprinkled with hot water.

If you accommodate others, you will be accommodating yourself.

A glutton is able to take off his skull in order to stuff himself more quickly with food.

Gods and immortals sometimes lose their swords.

Though gold dust is precious, when it gets in your eyes, it obstructs your vision.

To do good for ten years is not enough; do bad things for one day and it is too much.

Good deeds stay at home, bad deeds echo a thousand miles.

Even good news is bad news if it's false.

He who gossips behind my back is afraid of me; he who praises me to the face despises me.

The guilty party is the first to sue.

The heavy is the root of the light.

Honey in his mouth, knives in his heart.

Man is like a child born at midnight; when he sees the sun, he doesn't know that yesterday ever existed.

An honorable man is a majority of one.

A hundred is not much, but one is not little.

Better to have a modest but steady income than one thousand pieces of gold.

Indulgences have more victims than swords.

The palest ink is better than the best memory.

When you are involved you are bewildered, when you are not involved you see things clearly.

Jealousy arises often from a narrow heart.

In the presence of princes the cleverest jester is mute.

Stolen joys are always the sweetest.

Though the sword of justice be sharp, it will not slay the innocent.

Some people repay kindness with hatred.

Those who know do not tell;
those who tell do not know.

All laughter is a well of tears.

Lend money to someone who won't pay you back and he will hate you.

If luck is against you, even water will stick in your teeth.

The light of a hundred stars does not equal the light of the moon.

Take away the lips and the teeth get cold.

Honor and shame give birth to the same fear.

If luck comes, who comes not?
If luck comes not, who comes?

The three times liar is never again believed.

You buy land, you buy stones; you buy meat, you buy bones.

Medicine cures the man who is fated not to die.

No melon peddler cries, "Bitter melons."
No wine dealer says, "Sour wine."

Even the Goddess of Mercy sheds tears.

The miracle is not to fly in the air, or to walk on the water, but to walk on the earth.

Misfortunes never come alone.

Mockery is the flashing of slander.

The moon is not always round, the flowers do not always bloom, and men do not always have a happy reunion.

This is the one moment in ten thousand days.

If two men unite, their money will buy gold.

If you don't spend the small money, the big money will not come.

The name that can be named is not the eternal name.

Negligence is the stepsister of theft.

Ten night lights are not worth one lamp.

A hundred "no's" are less painful than one insincere "yes."

Even an old broom has its worth.

Opinions are like nails: the more often you hit them, the deeper they penetrate.

The past, the present, where do they end?
A thousand years are gone with the wind.

Patience is wisdom in waiting.

For those who can wait, time opens its doors.

A youth is to be regarded with respect. How do you know that his future will not be equal to our present?

Philosophy had its golden age when there were no philosophers.

A picture is worth ten thousand words.

Politics makes strange bedfellows.

He who praises himself stinks.

It is better to offer your prayers to the spirits than to man.

An ounce of prevention is worth a pound of cure.

Much property is a trap for the stupid.

After three days without reading, talk becomes flavorless.

A single untried popular remedy often throws the scientific doctor into hysterics.

A false report rides post.

False modesty is real pride.

Even though you have ten thousand fields, you can eat but one measure of rice a day.

A rich man must fear publicity like a pig that must fear its fatness.

When the rich lose weight, the poor starve.

Being in the right does not depend on having a loud voice.

A rumor goes in one ear and out many mouths.

Be skeptical; long garments can also hide big feet.

A scholar's ink lasts longer than a martyr's blood.

Practicing science and not loving men is like lighting a torch and closing your eyes.

The best kept secrets are those you keep for yourself.

Size is of the least importance. For a giant corpse only feeds more vultures.

He who smiles in all directions only gets wrinkles in his face.

Music in the soul can be heard by the universe.

Spectators have a better overview than the contestants.

There is no spoon that ever hurt the rim of a pot.

A very large square has no visible corners.

A starving man is not picky about his food.

The tranquil is the ruler of the hasty.

People who easily say "yes" are seldom faithful.

A good storyteller must be able to lie a little.

What is crooked, will stretch,
What is twisted, will be straightened.

If you see a strange thing and do not regard it as strange, its strangeness will vanish.

A little straw shows which way the wind blows.

Rascality has limits; stupidity has not.

The key to success isn't much good until one discovers the right lock to put it in.

The man who comes with a tale about others has himself an axe to grind.

It is not easy to steal where the landlord is a thief.

Temptation wrings integrity even as the thumbscrew twists a man's fingers.

Tenacity and adversity are old enemies.

Those who have free tickets to the theatre have the most criticism to make.

Those who have free seats at the play are the first to hiss.

A thief has more than two hands.

If you wish to know what most occupies a man's thoughts, you have only to listen to his conversation.

He that will thrive must rise at five.

The tongue is like a sharp knife: it kills without drawing blood.

Without traitors, the loyal do not stand out.

If you give a student one corner of a subject and he can't find the other three, the lesson is not worth teaching.

Not collecting treasures prevents stealing.

There are different truths: there is my truth, there is your truth and there is the truth.

Who does not trust enough will not be trusted.

The year long trial breeds ten years of rancor.

To persecute the unfortunate is like throwing stones on one fallen into a well.

Unhappiness conquers frightened souls; meanwhile, great minds tame unhappiness.

Everyone knows the usefulness of the useful, but no one knows the usefulness of the useless.

Half-full vessels slosh around, full ones do not.

For a villain, a warning is just a sigh in the wind.

Vinegar grows more pungent with age.

The one who first resorts to violence shows that he has no more arguments.

There is no cure for vulgarity.

To one who waits, a moment seems a year.

Want a thing long enough, and you don't.

A weapon is only loyal to the one who uses it.

It's not that the well is too deep, but rather the rope is too short.

A wheel is made of thirty spokes, but it is turned by the axis.

You can't stay at the top of the wheel of fortune forever.

To see and listen to the wicked is already the beginning of wickedness.

You win by not gambling.

The wine of your country is always good.

Good wine is the best way to iron out difficulties.

After praising the wine, they sell us vinegar.

As one lamp serves to dispel a thousand years of darkness, so one flash of wisdom destroys ten thousand years of ignorance.

Wisdom is the best weapon of war.

A woman who sells fans shields her eyes from the sun with her own hands.

Women hold up half the sky.

To tell a secret to a woman is like pricking a soap bubble.

The tongue of a woman is the sword that is never allowed to rust.

A wonder lasts but nine days.

You cannot make beautiful sculptures from rotten wood.

Square words won't fit into a round ear.

Words are empty, but the writing brush leaves traces.

Do your work, then step back.
The only path to serenity.

The world's affairs are but a dream in spring.

The world is doing fine when there is no news to talk about.

There is no such thing as a worthless person or a tree without roots.

By bending one yard, it will straighten into eight yards.

Practical Advice and Common Sense

If you are standing on the edge of an abyss, don't step back.

Active people never have louse bites.

Taking advantage of what is, we recognize the utility of what is not.

Hold back some goods for a thousand days and you will be sure to sell at a profit.

Don't do it on a rainy day if you have a chance to finish it on a sunny day.

While you should have something planned for not having it, don't wait until you don't have it to plan for having it.

If you lose an hour in the morning, you must spend the rest of the day looking for it.

If you strike someone with your fist, beware of a kick in return.

When you lift your hand to strike, you are three-tenths lower than your opponent.

Almond nuts come to those who have no teeth.

Of all the 36 alternatives, running away is best.

When you are very angry, don't go to a lawyer;
when you are very hungry, don't be a poet.

He who restrains his appetite avoids debt.

If you neglect your art for one day it will neglect you for two.

It's a sad athlete who has to win thanks to a dead rat under his girdle.

Bad luck is only what could not be avoided.

You can lean on a bamboo stick, but not on a rope.

Even a beggar will not cross a rotten wooden bridge.

Blessings do not come in doubles, but calamities do.

Do not stand with your right foot on one boat and your left on another.

Friend, do not try to borrow combs from shaven monks.

A good breakfast cannot take the place of the evening meal.

A Buddha made of mud cannot save himself when crossing the river.

When you go to buy, don't show your silver.

The cautious seldom err.

If today a chance you see,
accept at once; it's good for thee.

Clever people may be victims of their own cleverness.

The plan of the day is made in the morning.

Settle one difficulty, and you keep a hundred others away.

To be discrete is far more difficult than to be eloquent.

Disobedience is the mother of a whipped back.

It is easier to know how to do a thing than to do it.

The doctor who rides in a chair will not visit the house of the poor.

I dreamed a thousand new paths...I woke and walked my old one.

There is no economy in going to bed early to save candles if the result is twins.

O eggs, never fight with stones!

Enjoy yourself. It's later than you think.

It is not a failure to be down, but it is to stay down.

When you fall flat,
At least grab a handful of sand.

If you want to attract attention, start a fight.

Those who play the game do not see as clearly as those who watch.

If you always give, you will always have.

He who falls asleep while slandering wakes up gossiping.

If you would rather not kill the chicken, ask your guest: "Shall I kill a chicken for you?"

A person with a determined heart frightens problems away.

It is not easy to help; it is easy not to help.

To be human is easy, to be a human being is difficult.

He who does not believe in justice, must beware the evil that is in good.

Teach your descendants the two proper roads—literature and farming.

You cannot lose what you never had.

There are misers who become wasteful, but never a waster became a miser.

Money, in the hands of a bachelor, is as good as gone.

The mouth is the entry point of disease and the departure point for misfortune.

The one legged never stumble.

Opportunities multiply as they are seized.

There are three kinds of person that you must not challenge: civil servants, customers and widows.

Last night I made a thousand plans, but this morning I went my old way.

Great politeness usually means "I want something."

He who waits for the surplus to give to the poor will never give them anything.

Don't try to make predictions, especially those concerning the future.

The best way to avoid punishment is to fear it.

Minimize big problems by dividing them into several small ones.

Pottery and fine porcelain must not quarrel.

It is easy to get a thousand prescriptions but hard to get one single remedy.

Never eat in a restaurant where the chef is thin.

You cannot pick up salt with dry fingers.

When you say one thing, the clever person understands three.

Do not take the seeds and throw away the melon.

Do not offer an animal's skin when you can pay with linen.

Silence is a true friend who never betrays.

He who cannot sleep says his bed was badly made.

Smile three times a day and you won't need any medicine.

He who snores the loudest will be the first to fall asleep.

If you have done no wrong, you need not fear the knock on your door at midnight.

If you beat spice, it will smell the sweeter.

It is easier to go and steal for a thousand days than to protect your house against thieves for a thousand days.

Steal a bell with one's ears covered.

Never lift up a stone to let it fall on your own foot.

When you want to test the depths of a stream, don't use both feet.

People strive for high spirits as fire strives to become flames.

Don't talk unless you can improve the silence.

To talk much and arrive nowhere is the same as climbing a tree to catch a fish.

A teacher is someone who ploughs with his tongue to fill his little bowl with rice.

He who is thirsty dreams that he is drinking.

The thief is no danger to the beggar.

Tension is who you think you should be.
Relaxation is who you are.

He that will thrive must rise at five.

He who stands on his toes will not stand upright
for long.

Beware of him who has honey on his tongue and
a sword around his belly.

Don't trouble trouble until trouble troubles you.

What is not urgent must be done quickly in order to take care of the urgent things calmly.

Small winnings make a heavy purse.

Without a head wind, a kite cannot fly.

Three glasses of wine end a hundred quarrels.

If one word does not succeed, ten thousand are of no avail.

Bitter words and weak arguments never lead to a solution.

A bad word whispered will echo a hundred miles.

A good writer does not need a special pen.

Yesterday, today and tomorrow—these are the three days of man.

Conclusion

*T*HIS COLLECTION PROVIDES JUST A small look into the rich history of China's culture and its people. Widely regarded as innovative in industry, steadfast in belief, and committed to family and country in equal measure, their culture is a testament to one of the oldest and most fully developed countries in the world.

What we have tried to show in these pages is our appreciation for Chinese culture, as well as our desire to learn from their example. With the goal of providing our readers with a broader perspective on life and new, profound wisdom, it is our hope that you have enjoyed your time indulging in the bountiful history of China, and all that it has to offer.